SCIENCE SOLVES IT!

SAVING ENDANGERED PLANTS and ANIMALS

JAMES BOW

Crabtree Publishing Company

www.crabtreebooks.com

Crabtree Publishing Company
www.crabtreebooks.com

Author: James Bow
Project editor: Tom Jackson
Designer: Lynne Lennon
Picture researcher: Sophie Mortimer
Indexer: Kay Ollerenshaw
Managing editor: Miranda Smith
Art director: Jeni Child
Design manager: David Poole
Editorial director: Lindsey Lowe
Children's publisher: Anne O'Daly
Editor: Michael Hodge
Proofreaders: Adrianna Morganelli, Crystal Sikkens
Project coordinator: Robert Walker
Production coordinator: Katherine Kantor
Prepress technician: Katherine Kantor

This edition published in 2009 by
Crabtree Publishing Company

The Brown Reference Group plc
First Floor
9-17 St. Albans Place
London N1 0NX
www.brownreference.com

Copyright © 2009 The Brown Reference Group plc

Photographs:
BRG: p. 6 (bottom), 8–9
Corbis: Pieter Hugo: p. 22 (left); Steve Kaufman: p. 27 (top); Jeffrey Markowitz: p. 24–25; Michael Reynolds: p. 15; Patrick Robert: p. 25 (bottom); Rickey Rogers: p. 10 (left); Jeff Vanuga: p. 23 (right)
Rex Features: KPA: p. 28-29; MGM: p. 27 (bottom); Sipa Press: p. 28 (left)
Science Photo Library: James King-Holmes: p. 20 (left); Stephen J. Krasemann: p. 4 (right); U.S. Fish & Wildlife Service: p. 26
Shutterstock: Noam Armonn: p. 6–7; Kitch Bain: p. 4–5; Bob Blanchard: p. 18–19; Sebastien Burel: p. 18 (bottom), 20–21; Steve Byland: p. 25 (top); Janet Carr: p. 7 (bottom); Ferenc Cegledi: p. 22–23; Andraz Cerar: p. 7 (top); Sergey Dubrovsky: p. 9 (bottom); Bart Everett: p. 12–13; FloridaStock: p. 12 (bottom), 17 (right); Ieva Geneviciene: p. 24 (bottom); Eric Gevaert: p. 21 (bottom); Imageshunter p. 10–11; Mnoor: p. 13 (right); Bogdan Posteinicu: p. 13 (bottom), 17 (bottom); Russell Shively: p. 8 (bottom); Gina Smith: p. 14 (bottom); Manfred Steinbach: p. 16 (top); Nick Stubbs: p. 11 (right); Ruben Olavo Vicente: cover; Ke Wang: p. 29 (right); Kim Worrell: p. 14 (top)
Topfoto: ImageWorks: p. 16 (bottom); PA: p. 19 (bottom)

Every effort has been made to trace the owners of copyrighted material.

Library and Archives Canada Cataloguing in Publication

Bow, James, 1972-
    Saving endangered plants and animals / James Bow.

(Science solves it)
Includes index.
ISBN 978-0-7787-4170-1 (bound).–ISBN 978-0-7787-4177-0 (pbk.)

    1. Wildlife conservation–Juvenile literature. 2. Plant conservation–Juvenile literature. 3. Endangered species–Juvenile literature. I. Title. II. Series: Science solves it (St. Catharines, Ont.)

QL83.B69 2008   j333.95'16   C2008-905010-X

Library of Congress Cataloging-in-Publication Data

Bow, James.
    Saving endangered plants and animals / James Bow.
        p. cm. – (Science solves it)
    Includes index.
    ISBN-13: 978-0-7787-4177-0 (pbk. : alk. paper)
    ISBN-10: 0-7787-4177-X (pbk. : alk. paper)
    ISBN-13: 978-0-7787-4170-1 (reinforced library binding : alk. paper)
    ISBN-10: 0-7787-4170-2 (reinforced library binding : alk. paper)
    1. Wildlife conservation–Juvenile literature. 2. Plant conservation–Juvenile literature. 3. Endangered species–Juvenile literature. I. Title. II. Series.

QL83.B69 2009
333.95'16–dc22
                                        2008033789

Crabtree Publishing Company
www.crabtreebooks.com   1-800-387-7650

Published in Canada
Crabtree Publishing
616 Welland Ave.
St. Catharines, ON
L2M 5V6

Published in the United States
Crabtree Publishing
PMB16A
350 Fifth Ave., Suite 3308
New York, NY 10118

CONTENTS

ENDANGERED SPECIES

Could you kill the last member of an animal or plant **species**? People have. They did not mean to, they were just finding food for a meal or clearing space for a farm or house. But what they did resulted in an animal or plant becoming **extinct**—gone forever.

When European settlers first came to live on the east coast of North America in the 1600s, they needed to find food. Passenger pigeons (right) were easy to catch and their meat tasted good. There were a lot of passenger pigeons—they were probably the most common bird in North America. However, in the 1850s, people saw that there were fewer pigeons. Each year, the flocks of birds kept getting smaller. People tried to raise pigeons in zoos. This did not work, and on September 1, 1914, the last passenger pigeon died at the Cincinnati Zoo. Without meaning to, people had killed off the passenger pigeon species.

RED FOR DANGER

The International Union for Conservation of Nature (IUCN) has a list of species that have become extinct or are threatened with extinction. The IUCN estimates that as many as 16,000 species are in danger, with 2,500 in extreme danger. Some threatened species include the African elephant, the tiger, Atlantic cod, and the blue whale.

African elephants are in danger of dying out because people kill them for their huge ivory tusks.

Nature can cause problems for living things. For example, about 15,000 years ago North America was covered by a sheet of ice taller than a skyscraper. Most of the plants and animals died out.

When people are careless with the environment it is difficult for plants and animals to recover. In the early 1900s, cotton was the main crop of the southern United States. Then boll weevils attacked the crops and caused a disaster. The insect's favorite food is the cotton fruit and it found an endless supply. The fields were ruined. Growing just one crop—which scientists call **monoculture**—turned out to be a bad idea.

THE DEATH OF THE DINOSAURS

The disappearance of the dinosaurs was one of the biggest mysteries of science. Some suggest that a giant space rock hit Earth. The resulting dust cloud blanketed Earth and blocked out sunlight. Few plants could grow, and the mighty dinosaurs ran out of food.

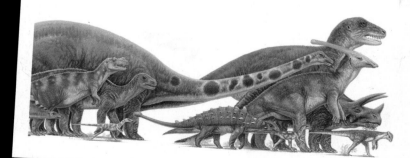

POLLUTION AND THE FOOD CHAIN

Mercury is a poisonous metal that gets into the air and water from coal-fired power plants and factories, but it does not stay there. Plants absorb the mercury from water and soil. The mercury then poisons fish and other animals that eat the plants.

Cotton is made from the fluffy white fibers that cover the fruits of cotton plants. Boll weevils eat the fruits so no fibers can form.

SHAKESPEARE'S STARLINGS

In 1890, American Eugene Scheifflin wanted to bring all the birds mentioned in William Shakespeare's plays to North America. He released 100 European starlings into New York's Central Park. The European starling spread quickly and took over nesting places from **native** birds, including the passenger pigeon. Today, starlings can be found throughout North America.

MAKING CONNECTIONS

Plants and animals rely on each other and their environment for survival. When this balancing act goes wrong the wildlife community collapses. Imagine if the rains failed in East Africa. It would be too dry for the grass to grow, and antelopes would starve to death. The lions that hunt the antelopes would also run out of food. Even hyenas, who eat dead bodies, would eventually starve, too. Wildlife can normally recover from such disasters.

Dinosaurs died out in a **mass extinction** along with half of all the species on Earth. However, mammals and birds survived and soon took over the world.

The largest mass extinction of all took place 250 million years ago when 80 percent of all sea life, including this trilobite, was wiped out.

However, some changes to the environment are so sudden and huge that species cannot recover and become extinct. Such events include **volcanic eruptions** and **asteroid** strikes, which create dust clouds that block sunlight and make the world dark and cold for years. Many species die out in an event called a mass extinction.

GOODBYE DINOS

In 1980, scientists discovered a thin layer of **iridium** dust (a very rare metal, found mostly in space rocks) buried in rocks all over the world. This layer of dust covered the surface of Earth 65 million year ago, just when the dinosaurs died out. This led scientists to believe a huge asteroid must have stuck Earth, wiping out the dinosaurs.

A NEW TIME

Geologists are scientists who study how Earth was made and how it is changing. Earth is 4.5 billion years old, and geologists divide its history into short sections. An epoch is a period of Earth's history that covers thousands of years. The current epoch is called the Holocene, which began 11,000 years ago at the end of the last **Ice Age**. Some scientists are now suggesting that a new epoch actually began about 300 years ago. In that time, people have become a new force that is changing the planet. They are building cities, creating piles of garbage (below), making species extinct, and changing the climate. Scientists have named the epoch the Anthropocene, which comes from the Greek word for "human."

9

HUMAN IMPACT

Humans have a big effect on the environment—but we are not the only ones. We hunt; wolves hunt. We cut down trees; beavers cut down trees. We are not doing anything other animals do not. We are just doing it too fast for the environment to recover. Humans have hunted several species to extinction and we are about to kill off thousands more.

Humans also take away **habitats**. We drain wetlands and cut down forests to make way for farms and cities. This robs animals of their homes. It also reduces the number of plants that are available to absorb **carbon dioxide**. This has made Earth hotter and is changing our weather.

> The Amazon rainforest is shrinking by the equivalent of 75 football fields every minute!

TREE TROUBLE

Farming wears out the land if it is not done carefully. Some farmers are forced to move to find new land, often burning forests to clear the way for food. The Amazon rainforest is shrinking by the equivalent of 75 football fields every minute!

KILLER WASTE

Humans also **pollute** the environment. We pump sewage into lakes and oceans, and poisonous gas into the air. People once thought the air and water would **dilute** waste and it would disappear. However, we now know that poisons stay in soil and water for years. Large amounts of poisons, such as mercury and lead, kill animals and make people sick. Everyone is exposed to tiny amounts of pollution every day.

THE GREENHOUSE EFFECT

A greenhouse stays warm because its glass lets the heat in but not out again. Earth's atmosphere does the same thing. Greenhouse gases, such as carbon dioxide, trap the Sun's heat around our planet. Without this "Greenhouse Effect," Earth would be a ball of ice. Humans have added carbon dioxide to the air by burning fuel. This traps more heat and appears to be making our weather more extreme.

Modern factories are designed to clean smoke and other waste to reduce the amounts of any poisons to safe levels.

IS THE ENVIRONMENT IMPORTANT?

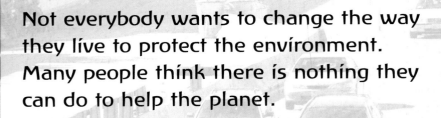

Not everybody wants to change the way they live to protect the environment. Many people think there is nothing they can do to help the planet.

Some argue that stopping activities that harm the environment would cost too many jobs. Others suggest that people have done too much damage already, and it is too late to save the planet. Humans are not separate from the environment. The risks of doing something to protect the planet are very small compared to the disasters that might occur if we do nothing.

Half of all air pollution in the United States comes from cars.

DDT DAMAGE

In trying to control nature, we sometimes make things worse. In the 1950s, the **DDT pesticide** was used to kill mosquitoes. These insects spread diseases such as malaria and yellow fever. DDT reduced these diseases, but it also killed fish and made it hard for birds to **breed**. Because of DDT, several species, including the bald eagle, nearly became extinct.

BANANA DISASTER

Did you have a banana at breakfast? Enjoy it because it might not be around much longer. Almost all bananas are of the Cavendish variety. The trees in the world's banana groves are closely related, and they all catch the same diseases. A **fungus** is attacking the Cavendish banana. It is feared this common banana may die out in the next ten years.

CROP FAILURE

The danger of reducing **biodiversity** is that we open the door for diseases or **parasites** to wipe out the remaining species. This could be a disaster. In the 1840s, a fungus called potato blight destroyed Ireland's potato crop. Potatoes were the Irish people's main source of food. A million people starved to death.

13

Most sea otters live on the coasts of Russia, Alaska, and Pacific islands, but small communities survive near Vancouver Island in Canada and Monterrey Bay in California.

EXAMINE THE FACTS

An **ecosystem** can be as small as a puddle. You might even have one in your home. Do you have a fish tank? Keep an eye on how the tank changes from day to day. Does it require cleaning very much? Natural ecosystems do not need cleaning. One animal's waste is another's food. In a fish tank, food is added and air is bubbled through it to keep the tank from getting stagnant. It is also important that pet cats are not allowed to join the ecosystem—they might eat all the fish!

OTTER IMPACT

The sea otter once lived along the entire Pacific coast of North America. Fur traders nearly hunted the otters into extinction. Then the Pacific Ocean started moving inland. Incredibly, the two events are connected. When the sea otters disappeared, the sea urchins they ate increased in number. The urchins then ate the forests of **kelp**. The kelp had sheltered beaches from the waves. Without the sea otter, the beaches **eroded** away.

LIVING IN GROUPS

Scientists describe a group of plants and animals that depend on each other as an ecosystem. People that study how ecosystems function are called **ecologists**. Ecologists can help predict what would happen if just a single species was to disappear from an ecosystem. For example, the gopher tortoise of the southeastern United States builds burrows that provide shelter for 360 other species. If the gopher tortoise becomes extinct, other species will suffer.

> When the number of sea otters decreased beaches were washed away!

MAKING MORE DESERTS

Plants store water for an ecosystem. Their roots absorb water from soil and slowly release it into the air. Without plants, any rain that falls soon trickles away and is lost. If goats or cattle are allowed to eat all the grass in a dry area, it becomes an empty desert. The soil dries into sand, which is useless for growing plants. The world's deserts are growing. In northern China (right), the edge of the desert has been covered in hay to stop the sand from spreading.

Banana plants do not grow from seeds. Instead, each one grows from a root belonging to another plant nearby.

MIRACLE PLANTS

A quarter of all prescriptions in the United States are for medicines whose **active ingredients** come from plants. The U.S. National Cancer Institute has identified 2,000 rainforest plants that can help fight cancer. Two drugs made from the Madagascar periwinkle (below) increased the survival rate of kids with **leukemia** from 20 percent to 80 percent. The periwinkle is now extinct in the wild and grows only on farms. We were lucky to have discovered the medicines before the periwinkle disappeared. Scientists are racing to find the next miracle plants— before they disappear forever.

GOING BANANAS?

Humans depend on the environment for food just as much as any other animal. Until the 1960s, most of the bananas eaten in the world were the Gros Michel variety. Then a fungus wiped out the crop. Today, the Cavendish banana that replaced the lost variety appears to have a similar problem. People do not survive on bananas alone.

But imagine what would happen if another disease destroyed the world's wheat or corn harvests. Millions of people would starve. Scientists are now warning about this **genetic erosion**. The variety of crops is falling fast as the world's farmers choose to grow the same varieties that produce the best harvests. The lack of variety makes all our food more **vulnerable** to attack from diseases, just like bananas.

> DDT made bald eagles lay eggs with very weak shells that cracked in the nest.

EAGLE THREAT

The United States took the bald eagle as its national symbol in 1782 when there were 25,000 eagles in the country. Loss of habitat and the use of DDT reduced that number to just 417 nesting pairs in 1963. DDT made the eagles lay eggs with very weak shells. Eggs cracked in the nest before the chicks were ready to hatch. DDT was banned in 1972, and the eagles' nesting sites are now protected. The birds have since made a comeback.

Monocultures, such as this huge wheat field, are easier to harvest than a field containing several crops. However, they are more at risk from disease.

The whooping crane was not as common as the passenger pigeon, but it also suffered from too much hunting and habitat loss. By 1941, there were only 23 of these birds left!

People took action. Some of them knew very little about birds, but they thought that it was wrong to let the species go extinct. Other people knew how and where the birds lived. Still others had the scientific knowledge so that proper studies and plans could be made. Working together, these different people, who we now call **conservationists**, stopped the hunting and protected whooping-crane habitats across North America. Some scientists bred the birds in zoos and then released them into the wild. The species is safe but there is still a lot to do—there are still only 300 whooping cranes in the world.

Whooping cranes spend the summer in northern Canada and fly south to Texas for the winter.

BISON HUNTING

Bison now live in small parks. They may be hunted so they do not eat all of the available food in the area. Native groups are sometimes allowed to hunt to maintain their traditional ways, which do not threaten the species.

PUBLIC LANDS

The United States has several different types of protected land:

National forests—land managed for timber harvesting and **recreation**.

Wilderness areas—motor vehicles and buildings are **prohibited**.

National parks—logging and mining are not allowed.

Wildlife refuges—managed to support the wildlife; limited amounts of hunting allowed.

National landscape monuments—Set aside for recreation, some hunting and animal grazing are allowed.

CLONING QUESTIONS

Could **cloning** be used to save endangered species? Dolly, the first cloned sheep, died at age six. Sheep usually live twice as long. Dolly was cloned from a six-year-old sheep. Was her lifespan cut in half because of this? The scientists who cloned her disagree: Dolly died from a common lung disease.

Bison are often called buffalos but they are only distantly related to cattle-like buffalos from Africa and Asia. Their closest relative is the European bison.

REAL LIFE

The Millennium Seed Bank Project based in Britain plans to collect seeds and plant specimens from 24,200 species worldwide. It is an insurance policy against extinction. If a plant species goes extinct, the seed bank can plant some of the stored seeds—even if **decades** have passed. It is not a perfect system, though. For one thing, the bank will store only about a quarter of the 100,000 plant species that are under threat worldwide.

FORCE OF LAWS

The Great Plains of the United States once shook under the feet of vast herds of American bison. However, the animal was hunted to near extinction in the 1800s. Thanks to conservation, the population has rebounded to half a million. The bison were saved when conservationists asked governments to rule that hunting bison was against the law. Laws do not always work. It is **illegal** to kill gorillas, but criminals continue to hunt them in Central Africa.

The laws that protect the North American wolf are opposed by some farmers. They say the animals kill **livestock** and should be shot.

LIVING SPACE

Even when hunting stops, many animals have nowhere to live. Their habitats are cleared to make way for cities, farms, and mines. The American bison is protected today in a number of national parks and wilderness areas in Canada and the United States. Other rare species are protected in other parks, including the bighorn sheep, prairie dogs, and the Mono Lake brine shrimp.

Bison were saved from extinction by a hunting ban.

CAREFUL BREEDING

The golden lion **tamarin** was saved from extinction by being raised in zoos. However, when the first zoo-born monkeys were released into the wild in Brazil, many fell out of the forest trees and died. After a life in a zoo cage with fixed logs and perches, the animals were not used to moving around in the swaying branches. The zoos changed their programs and the tiny monkeys were raised in real trees from then on.

RAISED IN CAGES

Sometimes a species can become so threatened that scientists step in to breed the plants and animals themselves. Animals bred in zoos grow up without facing the dangers of the wild, and can be released back into the wild when fully grown. **Captive-breeding** programs have been used to bring species such as the California condor back from the brink of extinction.

In 1987 there were just 19 California condors left. Thanks to a careful breeding program there are now more than 200.

FORMERLY EXTINCT

A program in South Africa is trying to breed a species that has become extinct! The quagga died out in 1883. Scientists know that quaggas were closely related to the plains zebra. The breeders choose zebras that look most like quaggas. Their children will look even more like members of the lost species. The nearest the project has come to producing a modern quagga is Henry (below).

Scientists are trying to breed quaggas, which became extinct in 1883!

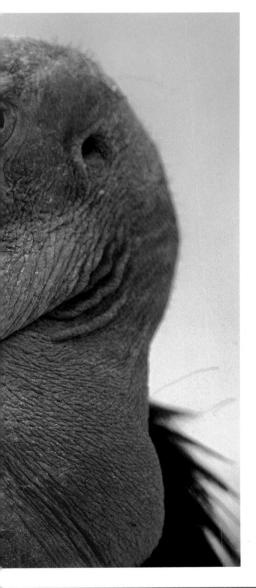

EXTINCT IN THE WILD

Some species survive only in zoos or in other protected areas. These precious animals have been saved from extinction, but for many there is nowhere safe in the wild for them to be released. One American species that is being returned to the wild is the black-footed ferret (right).

Captive-breeding can also have risks. If the animal population being bred is too small, **inbreeding** can occur, making the animals vulnerable to disease. Other animals are difficult to breed in captivity, especially if they are used to living in wide-open spaces or have complicated mating systems.

GETTING HELP

The black robin of the Chatham Islands of New Zealand was facing extinction when scientists tried to encourage the birds to breed. The birds were breeding too slowly, but scientists discovered that the black robins could double clutch—if a robin loses an egg, it will try again. Scientists removed the first eggs laid in a robin's nest and gave them to **foster parents** from another species. The rare robins laid more eggs, so two **clutches** of eggs would hatch each year.

People all over the world care about the environment around them and want to protect it. Experts figure out what needs to be done, but you do not have to be a scientist to look after the environment.

Does your school celebrate Earth Day? Earth Day started in the United States back in 1970. Since then, it has spread to many other countries around the world. Earth Day is always held in the middle of spring. One of the things you learn about Earth is that seasons do not happen at the same time all over the world. In North America, Earth Day is usually every April 22. In the **Southern Hemisphere**, the day is held during our fall—which is their spring.

WHAT CAN YOU DO?

You can protect the environment by changing the way you live. Use less electricity and water and avoid using harmful chemicals. Walk, cycle, or take public transit instead of getting driven to school. What you buy has a real impact on the environment. Think about **organic foods** or foods grown locally. What can you do today to start to make a change?

YOUR YARD

Do you have a lawn? Talk with your family and get them to help you change part of it from grass to a place for local wildflowers. Neatly trimmed grass needs a lot of water and chemicals to stay green. A wildflower garden can provide a home for birds and insects instead.

WORKING WITH PLANTS AND ANIMALS

If you want to works with plants and animals, then you will need to go beyond what you are learning in science class and get involved. Make a list of local groups from the phone book or the Internet, such as a conservation society or the **SPCA**. Talk with your friends, and volunteer to help in your local area.

A huge globe is part of an Earth Day event in Washington, D.C., when people celebrate the natural environment.

25

EXPERT PANEL

Saving the planet is a big job, and it takes a lot of experts to figure out the many things that people need to be doing. Biology is the study of life, but there are many different types of living things, and that means there are many different areas of biology. Botanists are experts on plants. People who study animals are called zoologists. Ecologists study ecosystems and look at how plants and animals live with each other. Geneticists study how living things vary from one another and figure out what it is that makes them different. Agronomists study soils and crops. Oceanographers learn about the oceans and seas. Foresters study trees and forests.

Wildlife rangers have many jobs and might work in a busy office in a city or be stationed in the wilderness.

RANGER WORK

Wildlife rangers protect both people and the environment. Rangers have many jobs and might work in a busy office in a big city or be stationed by themselves in the wilderness. They might be enforcing the boat speed limits in **lagoons** in Florida to protect the manatees in the water or **monitoring** polar bears in Hudson's Bay to stop illegal hunting. Rangers also look after visitors to national parks and wilderness areas.

Field biologists study rare foxes in California in order to figure out a way of protecting them better in future.

JOBS TO DO

Scientists study how wildlife is being affected by humans. Other people work to protect the environment, too. Park rangers make sure people obey wildlife laws; forestry technicians replant trees after bush fires or other disturbances. It is the job of education officers to teach everyone about the importance of **maintaining** wildlife areas. Environmental lawyers help make sure people, businesses, and even governments follow regulations that protect the environment.

STEVE IRWIN

Steve Irwin was an Australian wildlife expert who created the television series *The Crocodile Hunter*. He introduced many people to nature. Sadly, Irwin passed away in 2006. His wife Terri is continuing Irwin's conservation work through the Wildlife Warriors organization.

DIAN FOSSEY

Dian Fossey spent 18 years studying mountain gorillas in Rwanda, Africa. Her work was followed by *National Geographic* magazine, and Fossey wrote a book about it called *Gorillas in the Mist*. Many people thought gorillas were real-life King Kongs, but Fossey showed that these large **apes** were not aggressive, savage beasts. Fossey organized patrols to stop **poaching** and worked to protect their forests. Today the remaining mountain gorillas are protected by three national parks.

BE ORGANIZED

The biggest conservation organizations are run by governments. These include the U.S. Fish and Wildlife Service and the Canadian Wildlife Service. As government agencies, these services have a tough job—they must balance the interests of different people. Some people may want to keep a forest totally untouched. Others might want trails and roads to run through it to make it easier for people to travel around. Some people might want to cut down the trees for firewood or lumber.

PEOPLE POWER

Non-government organizations, such as the World Wildlife Fund (WWF) and Greenpeace, choose which problems they will work on. The WWF has projects in 100 countries. The U.S. Wildlife Conservation Society is older than the WWF, and has operated since 1895 out of the Bronx Zoo in New York City. It works to save wildlife and habitats by educating people at its **urban** wildlife parks. It runs a number of international projects, including a campaign to save the tigers of Asia.

RARE BEAR

In 1960, British scientist Sir Julian Huxley started the World Wildlife Fund (WWF). Today, the WWF is the largest conservation **charity** in the world with five million members. The giant panda (below) was chosen as the WWF's symbol, and today great efforts are made to protect this cute bear. However, some experts now suggest that saving the pandas is not important. Pandas do not play a big role in their ecosystem, and there are much larger and more urgent environmental problems.

Greenpeace members try to stop hunters from killing a whale. Hunting whales for meat is illegal, but some countries still do it.

GLOSSARY

active ingredients The parts of a medicine that work to cure an illness

apes Relatives of monkeys that do not have tails; gorillas and chimps are apes

asteroid Huge space rock

biodiversity The variety of plants, animals, and other species

breed To mate and produce offsrping

captive breeding A project that breeds rare animals in zoos

carbon dioxide An invisible gas produced when fuel is burned

charity An organization that is funded by money from the public

clutches A group of eggs that hatch into chicks

cloning Creating a baby animal with just one parent; the clone and parent have identical genes

conservationists A people who work to protect, or conserve, wildlife

DDT A kind of chemical for killing insects

decade A period of ten years

dilute To water down or thin out a substance

ecologists Scientists that study how ecosystems work and might change

ecosystem A group of living things that share an environment and depend on each other

eroded Gradually washed or worn away

extinct When all members of a species die off

foster parents Adults who look after children who are not related to them

fungus A living thing that is neither a plant or animal

genetic erosion A reduction in the variety of genes in crops, making crops too similar

habitats The place where plants and animals live

Ice Age A time when the world was colder and ice covered much of the surface

illegal Against the law

inbreeding When animals are too closely related to each to have healthy children

iridum A very rare metal

kelp Long, brown seaweed that grows in underwater forests near the shore

leukemia Cancer that affects the blood

livestock Animals, such as cattle, sheep, or chickens, raised for meat, eggs, or milk

lagoons Saltwater lakes that are connected to the sea

maintaining Looking after something so it always stays the same

mass extinction When a great number of species die out at the same time

monitoring Watching for and recording changes

monoculture A field growing just one crop

native Originally from the local area

organic foods Food that is grown without using any chemicals, such as pesticides

parasites Living things that survive by growing on or inside other plants or animals

pesticide Any chemical used to kill pests

poaching To hunt protected animals

pollute To add substances to the environment

prohibited Not allowed

recreation Fun activities, normally done outside

Southern Hemisphere The bottom half of Earth south of the Equator

SPCA Society for the Prevention of Cruelty to Animals

species A group of animals that all look very similar and can breed with each other

tamarin A small monkey from South America

urban In the middle of a city

volcanic eruption When lava, smoke, and gases are blasted out of a volcano

vulnerable At risk from something

FURTHER INFORMATION

Books

Endangered Species: Our Impact on the Planet by Malcom Penny.
Austin, TX: Raintree Steck-Vaughn Publishers, 2002.

Protecting Wildlife by Sharon Dalgleish. Philadelphia, PA: Chelsea House
Publishers, 2003.

Saving Endangered Animals with a Scientist by Judith Williams. Berkeley
Heights, NJ: Enslow Publishers, 2004.

Web sites

Canadian Wildlife Service:
http://www.cws-scf.ec.gc.ca

Global Seed Vault:
http://www.seedvault.no

IUCN Red List:
http://www.iucnredlist.org

Millennium Seed Banks:
http://www.kew.org/msbp/index.htm

Sea Watch Foundation:
http://www.seawatchfoundation.org.uk

U.S. Fish and Wildlife Service:
http://www.fws.gov

Wildlife Warriors:
http://www.wildlifewarriors.org.au

WWF:
http://www.worldwildlife.org

Printed in the U.S.A.